COVENANT
of CARE

COVENANT
of CARE

Maxine Lantz

WestBow
PRESS
A DIVISION OF THOMAS NELSON

WestBow Press books may be ordered through booksellers or by contacting:

WestBow Press
A Division of Thomas Nelson
1663 Liberty Drive
Bloomington, IN 47403
www.westbowpress.com
1-(866) 928-1240

Because of the dynamic nature of the Internet, any web addresses or links contained in this book may have changed since publication and may no longer be valid. The views expressed in this work are solely those of the author and do not necessarily reflect the views of the publisher, and the publisher hereby disclaims any responsibility for them.

Certain stock imagery © Thinkstock.
Any people depicted in stock imagery provided by Thinkstock are models, and such images are being used for illustrative purposes only.

ISBN: 978-1-4497-5641-3 (e)
ISBN: 978-1-4497-5640-6 (sc)

Library of Congress Control Number: 2012910607

Printed in the United States of America

WestBow Press rev. date: 9/21/2012

AUTHOR'S FOREWORD

I have called this booklet of poetry "Covenant of Care" because, due to the covenant in the blood of Jesus Christ, I know without a doubt that I rest in his care. I hope that these poems will give you some insight into what I believe is the true character of God and his son, Jesus Christ. I thank God for saving me, and I look forward to spending eternity with God and Jesus Christ.

I pray that these poems will edify the reader, and that those who know Christ as Saviour will be encouraged to continue their walk with him. For the reader that does not yet know Christ in this personal way, I pray that these words will lead you to the point in your life where you will accept Christ as your personal Saviour.

I would also like to take this opportunity to thank the keepers of my words. Each poem I write gets sent to my sister (Lynda Taylor), my husband Jim, my pastor and his wife (John & Cheryl Scorgie, who are also dear friends), and to another two friends (Carrol Ross and Joyce Lindsay). They are my biggest supporters, and I thank them for their love, loyalty and faithfulness.

Thank-you,
Maxine Lantz

Other Books By This Author:

Rhyming Revelation
Love On The Wing
Flights Of Fancy
Basking In The Son-Shine
Abundant Life

CONTENTS

A BLESSING

May the Lord answer you when you're in distress,
And may Jacob's own God protect you.
May all support be given from Zion's mount,
And offerings be acceptable too.
May God remember all of your sacrifice
And give you all that your heart desires.
May all of your plans meet with total success;
We will shout for joy when this transpires.
We'll lift up our banner in the name of our God
For no victory, without him, we'd claim.
There's no power in what man is able to do
But there's power in God's holy name.
May the Lord grant you all things that you ask.
May you know where all good things come from.
May you ever give praise to our God and recall
That from his holy hand blessings come.
His anointed, I know, our God rescues and saves.
From his holy hill, he gives them reply.
With the saving power of his righteous right hand,
His answers will come from on high.
Some trust in chariots and some in great steeds;
But on the name of our Lord do we call.
We will rise up, in grace, and we will stand firm;
They'll be brought to their knees and they'll fall.

A GIFT BY SPECIAL DELIVERY

I wasn't there when the Gift arrived.
It was laid on a bed of hay.
The angels announced that the Gift had come
And then without delay
The shepherds left their flocks in the field
And went to Bethlehem town
To see the world's most wondrous Gift
Who from heaven's great heights had come down.
The Magi came with their presents there;
They came from a country far.
They brought their gifts upon camels' backs
And followed the shining star.
They found the Gift in a stable,
A place where cattle stirred,
And knelt before the Gift and gave
Gold, frankincense and myrrh.
King Herod did not want the Gift;
He saw it as a threat
And killed the babies under two
Without a hint of regret.

I'd heard the story of the Gift
Throughout the years much-told
And all the things that happened then
To make history unfold.
I never felt the Gift was mine
As I lived upon this earth.
But the day I repented of my sins
My gift was second birth.
The Gift that had lain upon that hay
Atoned for my sin and shame
And then I noticed in the Gift
Amazingly . . . my name!

The Gift just had been waiting
For me to see at last
That all the years of sin and shame
Were forgotten in the past.
And now I know the Gift is love;
It is mercy and it's grace
And it started when Christ came to earth
To a lowly stable place.

A MOTHER'S MEMORIES

Christ hung, bruised and badly beaten, upon dark Calvary's tree.
He'd willingly walked Golgotha's way to gain man's liberty.
His mother, Mary, watched her son; she could not hold her tears.
She could not stop the memories of His earthly thirty years.
She remembered when the angel told that she would be with child.
She said that she would do God's will in a voice so meek and mild.
She thought of that first Christmas day when her son arrived on earth,
How the shepherds told that a heavenly choir proclaimed His royal birth.
And then the wise men came to Him with gifts of worth untold -
Some myrrh, and then some frankincense and gifts of purest gold.
Her mind returned to his childhood days as He grew into a man,
And went about His earthly tasks to fulfill His Father's plan.
She thought of that Canaan wedding when water turned to wine;
It was only at her bidding that He'd performed that act divine.
And now she saw Him hanging on the cross, with thorny crown;
His hands and feet and side were pierced and His scarlet blood flowed down.
She remembered when, as a little boy, those hands had been at rest
As He slept upon his pillow, and how she had been blessed
When sometimes He would grasp her face and look into her eyes,
And say, "I love you, Mommy!". Those times were Mary's prize.
She remembered how His feet would race along the street at play,
And how she stored up in her heart all the moments of each day,
For she had always recalled that the angel said He'd die
In order that, with sacrifice, man's hell-damned soul He'd buy.
She thought of His disciples, who were like brothers to her son,
And knew how much they'd miss Him when the torture was all done.
He whispered, "Father, it is done." through a voice racked with great pain;
She knew that with those final words, she'd not hear His voice again.
Her loss was more than she could bear and anguish filled her soul
As she looked upon the son she'd borne, His body turning cold.
But, in that moment of great loss, her comfort came to mind
That when she slipped from earth down here, her Son again she'd find.
She'd share eternity with Him, and all the saintly throng
And praise and laud and honour for her son would be the song
That all would sing in heaven. That thought helped bring her peace
For she knew that Jesus' love for her would never, ever cease.

A NEW PATH

I'm walking a new path, Lord, my feet have never trod.
I know you won't desert me. You told me that, O God.

You called my lifemate home, Lord; he walks on earth no more.
My heart delights he's there, Lord, but aches right to the core.

For I miss his smile and presence, his humour and his ways.
The memories that I hold, Lord, sustain me all these days.

I know that you walk with me. I know that you are here.
You hold me when I cry, Lord, and shed my many tears.

And when the day is over and I climb in bed alone,
I feel this loss so strongly, my heart seems made of stone.

But your voice of love comes to me, and whispers in my ear,
"I'm here with you, my precious child, and you have naught to fear.

For I'll walk with you forever, near waters deep and still,
And comfort you in sorrow. Your life with love I'll fill.

And when you reach my mansion, and see your lifemate there,
You'll know I kept my promise, and kept you in my care."

Your words, Lord, will sustain me in days of joy and tears.
My hope will be fulfilled by you throughout remaining years.

And when I live in heaven and your glory's fully shown,
I'll say "My Counselor sustained me, and I never walked alone."

ABUNDANT GRACE

The harvest table groaned beneath the heavy weight
Of all the great abundance. The sight was really great!
The fruits of man's hard labour and God's abundant grace
Were placed upon the table in this October harvest place.

The wheat lay golden on the stock, some fruit lay right beside
And yet I knew their being there meant something in them died.
For taken from their source of life, whether branch or vine or ground,
They had to die so that in them God's potential would be found.

The wheat to flour and then to meals, the fruit perhaps to pies.
I realized then to fulfill God's plan, these things had had to die.
But then a greater thought came to me, it took me by surprise
That I like them, had died to self, to claim God's heavenly prize.

And yet, the difference in my life is I, each day, remain
With the one that gives me life each day and who my life sustains.
Whereas the fruit and wheat must die to meet God's daily plan
The plan he has for me is done when with his son I stand

And meet potential put in me before the world began
To love my God and all the world. What an awesome, holy plan!
So when I see the bounty that is piled here in this place
I know my life's the harvest that puts a smile upon God's face.

AMAZING GRACE

Amazing Grace! I love those words
That tell of blinded sight restored.
A hell-bound soul so full of sin
Is now redeemed forevermore.
Amazing Grace! Joy fills my heart
When I remember Calvary's cross -
A second birth, a second chance –
I know my soul won't suffer loss.
Amazing Grace! What worth I have
Bestowed on me from God's own Son.
I'll ever praise Him for His love,
His gracious mercy, all He's done.
Amazing Grace! I am reborn -
A sinner saved from hell's harsh fire.
I have His peace and joy that calms
My worries when the world conspires.
Amazing Grace! When I'm no more
And up to heaven my soul will rise,
Then life with Christ and God will start.
My soul will live when my body dies!
Amazing Grace! I'll sing those words
When I see Jesus, face-to-face,
And thank Him humbly for His love,
His mercy and amazing grace.

BECAUSE OF LOVE

Because of love, you left the realm of glory up on high,
And came to earth, a helpless babe, man's sin-filled soul to buy.
You would not pay with gold or gems, but with your precious blood.
Repentant hearts would find new life in that healing, cleansing flood.

Because of love, you walked on earth and fulfilled the Father's plan;
Your pain-filled death on Calvary's cross would redeem the soul of man.
When he would call upon your name, man's soul would be set free.
Your gift of mercy, love and grace would come with liberty.

Because of love, you walked each step up Calvary's cruel way,
Endured the beatings and the scorn they heaped on you that day.
You never called your angel hordes to take you off that cross;
You knew without blood being shed, mankind would all be lost.

Because of love, you hung and bled and saw the Father turn away;
He could not look upon the sin you bore for us that day.
You whispered, "It is finished", and then you breathed your last.
All sins of mankind were atoned – for future, present, past.

Because of love, you lay stone cold in the dreary, stony tomb,
But in your resurrection hour, your glory filled that room.
Your death atoned for mankind's sin, but when you rose in might,
Eternity was gained for those who move from darkness to God's light.

Because of love, my soul has found a Friend and Redeemer King.
There's naught so precious to my soul. No, not one single thing.
I call the King my brother and I call the King my Lord.
I hear his voice whene'er I pray and read His precious Word.

Because of love Christ has for all, you too can know His peace,
His joy, His mercy, and His grace, and love that will not cease.
A true repentant heart is what you bring and lay it at the cross.
His blood will cleanse and purify and discard all the dross.

Because of love, He'll take your life and make it clean as new.
You'll never find yourself alone, for He'll always walk with you.
In every situation, whether day or darkest night,
He'll hold your hand and dry your tears for you're precious in His sight

He's sitting at His Father's side, to intercede for man,
For between God and sinful man, Christ Jesus is the span
That stretches to the earth below from the heights of heaven above.
Eternity awaits those who believe, and it's all because of love.

BREAD AND LIFE

"Jesus answered, "It is written: 'Man does not live on bread alone, but on every word that comes from the mouth of God."

Matthew 4:4 NIV

In the opinion of many on this earth, we daily sit at tables replete with every choice morsel that could ever be desired. Through our eyes, the meals are meager and sometimes considered less than substantial or sufficient. We take the food on our tables for granted, and forget that all we have has been given to us by a great God, who loves us beyond human understanding. Through their eyes, our daily meals are viewed as feasts for the eyes and the stomachs.

While we ask, "What shall we have for supper tonight?", many in this world are asking "Will I eat tonight?". What we dispose of as scraps could be seen as delicacies to those who watch from afar with bloated and grumbling stomachs. They think "what a waste".

It is the same for spiritual food. Many in the world do not even know that they are suffering from spiritual hunger pangs. They don't realize that the food they are feasting on, all the things of the world, is detrimental to their spiritual health. This decline in spiritual health very often leads to spiritual death.

However, there are also many that do realize their total or partial lack of spiritual food. Many people in other parts of the world feed on anything spiritual that comes into contact with them, whether it be a radio broadcast, a Bible to be shared, or just communication with another believer. Whereas we, in our spiritual affluence, feast on God's word in many different versions, with radio broadcasts, as well as books written by Biblical scholars and other well-known Christian leaders. We have available to us a veritable Christian cornucopia.

We have so much that, as so often happens, we take our bounty for granted, and never consider just how blessed we are. We take for granted the fact that we can feast on God's word without fear of reprisal or repercussion, and believe that the spiritual food that we crave will always be available to meet our needs. We do not realize that all we have could be taken away from us in the blink of an eye.

How would you feed your soul if the food you now fill it with were to be taken away? How would you satisfy that deep inner hunger for God's word? As the Bible says, "Thy word have I hid in mine heart". This is the only way to keep the food that is essential to our spiritual life available, no matter the economic or political system in which we are living. Memorizing Scripture is the only way to ensure that you will always have a steady supply of spiritual food, and even to be able to give that same spiritual food to someone who is hungering for it.

Crumbs of physical food will not sustain life for any length of time. However, even "crumbs" of the Bread of Life can, and will, sustain spiritual life.

BY PRAYER AND PETITION

"Do not be anxious about anything, but in everything, by prayer and petition, with thanksgiving, present your requests to God. And the peace of God, which transcends all understanding, will guard your hearts and your minds in Christ Jesus."

Philippians 4:6-7 NIV

As you rest in the love of Jesus, the King,
Do not be anxious about anything.
With humble thanksgiving, give God all the praise;
To God and Jesus, holy anthems raise.
Your prayers and petitions present to Him
Who, in His great power, can do all things.
The peace of God that we cannot understand
Will comfort for you are held in God's hand.
Your mind will be guarded in God's only son.
You'll look back in wonder at what He's done.
By prayer and petition, present your requests
And God's holy answer will always be best.
And never be anxious, or worry or fret
When on the Lord Jesus, your heart and mind's set.

CALVARY'S CONSEQUENCE

I know that I can't walk your way unless I understand
Just how your death on Calvary fulfilled salvation's plan.

You paid the debt for all my sin and didn't count the cost.
The sins of all mankind you bore as you hung there on the cross.

Your death upon that cruel tree was slow and filled with pain,
And yet you stayed there just for me to cleanse my sin's dark stain.

I pray that I will never fail to thank you for your grace
Extended down from Calvary when you hung and took my place.

I know I'll never understand how much you loved my soul.
Your death was just the start of my dark heart becoming whole.

And I will tell the world at large just how you cared for me,
And showed how much you loved me so by hanging on that tree.

But that alone could not prevent my soul from searing hell.
There's so much more to comprehend, and so much more to tell.

They laid you in that stone cold tomb; what a truly awful hour!
But, on the third day, you arose in your resurrection power.

And that's what saved my soul from hell, and that's what I recall
When Satan whispers in my ear and tries to make me fall.

I tell him that you've beat the grave and death no more has sting.
I tell him that you are my Lord, my Savior and my King.

He flees because he knows his end has already been ordained,
But Satan will still try to win though he knows it is in vain.

But he cannot steal the joy and peace that only comes from you,
And the love that had you hanging will always shine so true.

CHRIST IS A BRIDGE

"Therefore he is able to save completely those who come to God through him, because he always lives to intercede for them."

Hebrews 7:25 NIV

All those who come to God in faith
Christ will completely save.
No fear or condemnation,
No victory for the grave.
He is man's bridge to access God;
He intercedes for man.
Without him, man would go to hell;
But Christ finished God's great plan.
When we yield up repentant hearts
And Christ takes us as His own,
It's then that God's great grace is given
And His great love is shown.
We're welcomed as a royal child-
The offspring of a king-
We need not ask for one thing more
For we have everything.
Each day He'll walk beside us,
We'll never be alone
Secure in the great knowledge
That our sins have been atoned.
Our hearts have been washed white as snow;
We're given second birth.
Our lives have been renewed and cleansed
And our soul's been given worth.
It's true that once we're given grace
Then grace we must bestow
On those that hurt us or betray,
On those we do not know.
For Christ should be our model
In the life on earth He lived,
When He gave love for scorn and pain
And was able to forgive.

CROWNING GLORY

As I approached the throne of grace, the King was sitting there.
I noticed that He wore a crown; it glinted in the air.
His face was shining like a star; His glory shone without.
He was the King of Heaven – of this there was no doubt.
But as I closer drew to Him, my eyes beheld a change.
His crown and face began to shift. I thought that it was strange.
His golden crown began to change into a thorny crown
His face, that first appeared so fair, was scarred and blood flowed down.
What caused this change I could not think, but then a thought took place.
Without the scars and flowing blood, I would not know His grace.
I would not know the peace and joy that daily floods my soul.
I would not know His cleansing power that made my spirit whole.
I could not claim Him as my King, availed of His great power,
If He had not defeated death in His resurrection hour.
My King sits on the throne of grace, Son of God and Son of Man.
He suffered death on Calvary and fulfilled salvation's plan.
So, wrapped up in His deity is His fateful human end.
This gives me the assurance with Him, eternity I'll spend.
He is my King Redeemer, who sits on heaven's throne,
But He's also Calvary's champion who claimed me as His own.

DEATH IS VANQUISHED

"Where, O death, is your victory? Where, O death, is your sting?" The sting of death is sin, and the power of sin is the law. But thanks be to God! He gives us the victory through our Lord Jesus Christ."

1 Corinthians 15:55-57 NIV

Where, O Death, is your victory?
Where, O Death, is your sting?
You, O Death, have been vanquished
By Jesus Christ, the King.

For sin is the sting of you, Death,
And the power of sin is the law.
But Jesus Christ has now triumphed
And you'll be cast into hell's maw.

Our God is due all our praises
For all that he has done,
By granting us the victory
Through Jesus Christ, his son.

And we'll glory in salvation.
With loud voices, we will sing,
"Where, O Death, is your victory?
Where, O Death, is your sting?"

DESERVING, BUT DELIVERED

I stood before the Judge's bench
Without a hope I'd win.
I knew the Judge would sentence me
For the greatness of my sin.

And just before the gavel hit
And I knew I would be lost,
A voice said "Set him free, I say,
For I have paid the cost."

I turned and noticed Christ, the King,
Who stood for all to see.
And then I saw the nail-scarred palms
As He held them out to me.

"I hung on Calvary's cruel cross.
I wore the crown of thorns.
When my Father turned His face away
I was left there, all forlorn."

I then recalled, when as a boy,
I'd heard that Christ had died
To save mankind from his dark stains.
That's why He was crucified.

He read my thoughts and added this,
"The grave didn't hold me long.
I stole the victory from the grave
And sang resurrection's song."

I could not see why He had died
To save a wretch like me,
But I yielded up my heart to Him
And my soul knew liberty.

He spoke directly to the Judge,
And His words were meek and mild,
He said, "Father, let this man go free
For he is now your child.

He's named me as his lord and king,
And humbly bowed his knee."
The Judge's gavel hit the block -
"You can set the prisoner free."

What a truly glorious time that was,
When Christ came to my defence
And gave me life, abundant, free
And a heart that has been cleansed.

DO NOT FEAR FOR I AM WITH YOU

"So do not fear, for I am with you; do not be dismayed,
for I am your God. I will strengthen you and help you;
I will uphold you with my righteous right hand."

Isaiah 41:10 NIV

Do not fear for I am with you.
Be not dismayed for I'm your God.
I will strengthen you and help you.
I will guide each step you'll trod.
And when there is time of danger,
I need you to understand
That I always will uphold you
With my own righteous right hand.
There will never be a kingdom,
Not a man and not a throne
That can ever take you from me
For I've claimed you as my own.
As a father loves his children
With a love that will not end,
My love never will be withdrawn.
On this fact, you can depend.
So, my Child, walk through each day
With the knowledge of my care.
And no matter where you journey
I will always be right there.
There's no time, no situation
That can ever change my love.
And we'll share a sweet communion
When your soul soars high above.
But, for now, you must remain there
While you do just what I ask.
With my power availed to you, Child,
You'll accomplish any task.
Just remember that I love you,
And I'll always be right near.
So do not be dismayed, Child.
I'm your God, so do not fear.

DON'T GRIEVE WHEN I LEAVE

I hear the angels singing.
I see Jesus at the gate.
But before I go, my loved ones,
There's a story to relate.
I was born a child of heaven
A great gift from God above.
But my story doesn't end there
Thanks, in part, to God's great love.
For Satan's world came calling
And it slowly took its toll.
I was in a battle royal
For the devil craved my soul.
But the Lord, in his great mercy,
Kept me out of Satan's snare
And he raised me up in victory
And held me tightly in his care.
For God's promised me a mansion
When at last he calls me home,
And I want to take possession
And this world no more to roam.
When I enter Jesus' presence
There will be no strife nor pain.
Your love is what I'm leaving,
But eternity's my gain.
So miss me just a little
While you spend your time down here
And when we're reunited
Up in heaven, then I'll cheer.
For we'll spend our time there praising
Our dear Lord with all our might,
And we'll spend our time together
Basking in our Saviour's light.

EASTER STORY RETOLD

You never offered rebuttal
As the charges were read out to you
They scoffed and hurled insults
And taunted "Behold the King of the Jews".
They accused you of stating that you were a king,
And Caesar's taxes you would not pay.
When Pilate asked "Are you the king of the Jews?"
You answered "It is as you say."
Then Pilate passed you to Herod
Because you came there from Galilee.
Herod was pleased to confront you
Because a miracle he wanted to see.
When you would not answer his questions,
You were ridiculed and mocked by the guards
An elegant robe was placed on your back,
But their intention was clear by their words.
Then they brought you right back to Pilate,
Who said that he just could not see
Why the charges had been brought against you.
But the wild crowd didn't agree.
"Release Barrabas and crucify Christ"
They shouted over and over again.
Pilate said he washed his hands,
And of your shed blood he'll have no blame.
They beat you and cast lots for your clothing
As Scripture said that they would.
You never called down your legions of angels.
As God's Son, I know that you could.
You suffered the cruel crucifixion –
You were nailed to that old rugged tree.
Crown of thorns pierced your head,
And the nails pierced your hands and your feet.
You said "Father, forgive them. They know not what they do."
As you hung on the cross between thieves.
The crowd taunted, "If he is the Christ of God, as he says,
Let him come down and then we'll believe."

One criminal told you to save yourself
And save him and the other thief too
But the other thief rebuked him, and said
"Listen to what I tell you.
We must pay the debts our deeds deserve.
It is right that we're punished this way.
But this man is innocent, has done nothing wrong".
And then I heard that thief say,
"Remember me when into your kingdom you come."
And you said in a pain-wracked voice,
To the contrite thief on the cross you said
"Today you'll be with me in paradise".
Then the day turned so dark that no one could see,
And the darkness lasted three hours.
And the temple curtain was torn in two,
Top to bottom, showing God' power.
Then you called out in a loud voice,
"Father, I commit my spirit into your hands."
And as soon as you'd finished uttering these words,
I heard you breathe your last.
Then Joseph of Arimathea,
A good and an upright man,
Asked Pilate for your body,
And Pilate said "You can".
So they placed you in that brand-new tomb,
Wrapped in death clothes of linen white,
And mourned the loss of their Teacher and Friend.
No more would you be in their sight.
But the tomb could not hold you and in power you arose,
And stole victory from Death's bony hands.
For your Resurrection ensures eternal life
For all those who abide by God's plans.
And I know when my time here is finished,
And I see you, Dear Lord, face to face,
I will worship and thank you, with all of my heart,
For taking this poor sinner's place.

FAITH LIKE A MUSTARD SEED

*"If you believe, you will receive whatever
you ask for in prayer."*

Matt. 21:22 NIV

With faith like a mustard seed, there's naught you can't do.
In prayer, when you ask, God will always bless you.
Just say to the mountain, "Go down to the sea!"
And the mountain will rise up at your decree.
King David when faced with a giant in his path,
Well knew that with God there, the giant could not last.
A sling and some small stones, and a faith that was staunch
Allowed him the victory as his slung stones he launched.
And Goliath fell dead and he paid for his sin
Of blaspheming the Lord's name, and believing he'd win.
And what seems impossible, and can't come to pass
Will seem like a miracle when it happens at last.
For our God is a big God, whose power and might
Can never be stopped, not by day or by night.
No kingdom or power can ever prevail
For with faith in our great God, we won't ever fail.
And it needs understanding that with faith like a seed
All things can be done, for that's all that you need.

FOLLOW ME

Then he said to them all: "Whoever wants
to be my disciple must deny themselves and
take up their cross daily and follow me.

Luke 9:23 NIV

You've chosen me in my weakness;
In you alone is my strength.
So, Lord, let me stay close beside you
As we travel along my life's length.
Clear away all that would separate us
Until the self in me disappears.
May your holy righteousness and love
Be the only things that shine clear.
Lord Jesus, as you lead me each day,
May I walk ever closely behind
So each step I take on your narrow path
In your footprints may I find.
So closely may I walk with you
That the dust from your steps trod
Will fall on me ere it hits the ground.
This I ask of you, my God.
May I walk within your shadow
And not be left behind in the sun,
For the sun will scorch me and cause me
To give up the race ere it's run.
May those that look there upon us
See you in your glory and might.
May they also see you within me
For that is just fitting and right.
May I follow, Lord, in your footsteps
So that all the world's people see
What a blessing's received in obeying
The words that you said, "Follow me!"
And when I slip this poor flawed earth
And look on Jesus' face,
I'll thank him for salvation's joy
And forgiveness by God's grace.

GIVE THANKS TO THE LORD

Give thanks for Christ's body on Calvary's tree.
Give thanks for the blood that flowed down.
Give thanks for the hope of eternity's gain –
A mansion, a robe and a crown.

Give thanks for the food on your table each day.
Give thanks for the people you love.
Give thanks for the love you receive in return,
Especially from God up above.

Give thanks for the gifts that you have in your life.
Give thanks for the fact that you can
Give thanks for what God has bestowed upon you –
Grace and mercy we can't understand.

Give thanks for the fact that God grants you each breath.
Give thanks for creation around.
Give thanks for the glorious hope that you have
That is in God and Christ only found.

Give thanks for the Father who reigns up above.
Give thanks for the Son who came here.
Give thanks for the Spirit, our helper and guide.
It's the Trinity we hold most dear.

GOD AND GOD ALONE

Who laid the earth's foundations?
It was God and God alone.
He laid a line to measure the earth;
He laid its cornerstone.
In the heavens, God ordained
The sun and the moon to hang
While all the angels shouted for joy
And the stars their praises sang

Who shut up the sea behind a door
When it burst from the womb?
Who made clouds for its garments,
And wrapped it dark, like a tomb?
God set all its limits and set its doors
And all its bars in place:
"Here you may come, no further"
Was God's command to its waves.

Who gives orders to the morning?
Who shows dawn its place
That it takes earth by the edges
And out the wicked shake?
God formed the features of the earth
Like some clay under a seal.
The wicked are denied their light
As God's power is revealed.

Who journeyed to the springs of the sea
Or walked the ocean depths?
Who's seen the gates of death
And the gates of the shadow of death?
God has done this and so much more;
Our minds can't comprehend.
He knows the way to the abode of light,
And where the darkness ends.

Who knows where all the snow is stored
Or the storehouses of hail?
Where does the lightning come from?
Who starts the windy gale?
God cuts a channel for the rain,
And gives the thunderstorm a path
To satisfy a desolate wasteland
And make it sprout with grass.

Who knows the father of the rain?
Who births the drops of dew?
God knows whose womb gives birth to ice,
And the frost from heaven, too.
He can bind the beautiful Pleiades
And loose Orion's cords.
The constellations, in their seasons,
The sovereign God brings forth.

Who can know the laws of heaven?
Who can oversee the earth?
God alone knows all these things,
And creation sings His worth.
He commands the bolts of lightning;
To Him they give report.
He names their destination
To the south, east, west and north.

Who has wisdom to count the clouds?
Who can open heaven's store
Of water when the ground is dry?
God can do this and more.
He provides the prey for lioness
And the raven's young are fed.
All nature in its processes is,
Without a doubt, God-led.

GOD'S BEST FOR MY GOOD

Before all the ages had been given birth
God had already bestowed on me worth.
A daughter, a princess, a child of the King
His praise through eternity I'll gladly sing.

His love for his children never wavers or fails,
In times on the mountain or down in the vales.
In times of rejoicing and times of despair
We rest in the arms of our Father who cares.

He constantly shows us just how much He loves
In a myriad of ways, His faithfulness proves.
As a sign to us all, He sent Jesus below
So to this lowly earth His great love could be shown.

And Jesus, in answer to His father's plan
Died on Calvary's cross to save sinful man.
And then rose on the third day as He said he would.
God gave us His best for the poor sinner's good.

GOD'S GRACE IN REDEMPTION

". . . for all have sinned and fall short of the glory of God, and are justified freely by his grace through the redemption that came by Christ Jesus."

Romans 3:23-24 NIV

Believers come to Jesus Christ
Because they know their state
As sinners, vile, condemned, unclean
And yet they're shown a way.
For though man falls short of his glory,
God knew what needed done.
He planned the perfect sacrifice
In the body of his own son.
For God, in his great love for us,
Prepared salvation's plan
To cleanse, restore and make as new
The soul of sinful man.
Christ bore the stripes upon his back
And thorny crown upon his head.
God's son, our Lord, went to the cross
And hung there in our stead.
God's grace was given freely
Through the redemption through his son
Whose work on earth was finished,
When Christ said "It is done".
God's grace has justified us.
We no longer live in sin.
We have the quiet assurance
That, on death, we'll enter in
The presence of our God and Christ,
And we'll share eternity.
We carry that one hope with us
In our salvation, great and free.

GOD'S VALENTINE

The world says that chocolate and flowers can prove
To the one that you care for your undying love.
A necklace, a pendant, a diamond or two
Will cause your true sweetheart to keep loving you.

With red hearts and pink hearts, and Cupid with bow
The world says that this way your love you can show.
The cost of the card or the gift is the price
But it doesn't involve a great sacrifice.

But God, in His wisdom, had a much better plan
To show love and mercy to earth's sinful man.
He gave up his first-born, the true Prince of Peace
To show to earth's people His love that won't cease.

Christ came to this earth in the form of a babe
Love lay in a manger on a soft bed of hay.
He grew into boyhood and then into a man
Then started His ministry to complete God's love plan.

He suffered a horrible death on the cross.
God ensured that all sinners need not remain lost.
For the blood that was shed from his hands, side and feet
Was the colour of cleansing, and made God's plan complete.

For the red blood that flowed made my sinful heart white
When I knelt at the cross and with God I got right.
Then I knew that the Valentine sent from above
Sealed my hope for salvation, and showed God's holy love.

GOD'S WAY IS PERFECT

"As for God, his way is perfect; the word of the LORD is flawless. He is a shield for all who take refuge in him."

Psalm 18:30 NIV

God's way is perfect, and I trust in His laws.
His word is forever without any flaw.
To those who take refuge in Him and don't yield,
He is a mighty omnipotent shield.

God's way is perfect, and I know it's true.
I've seen the great things that my God can do.
His way is righteous, and holy and just.
To my God, Him only, I offer my trust.

God's way is perfect; it's simple and plain.
And if we obey it, our lives He'll sustain.
Though death claim this body, I'll live evermore
With my God forever on His golden shore.

God's way is perfect; there's none can compare.
I rest so securely in God's loving care.
And each day forever as this globe I trod,
I'll tell just how perfect is the way of my God.

GOD WILL SUPPLY ALL YOUR NEEDS

There's never a moment when you're far from God's mind.
His grace, love and His mercy each minute you'll find.
He'll be right beside you, and each day you'll see
His power displayed and His mercy, so free.

God will supply all your needs every day.
God will lead you in peace as you travel His way.
God will help you, in love, to keep Satan at bay.
Our God will supply all your needs.

The need may be major or minor in scope;
Our God will supply what you're needing to cope.
Your body and spirit He'll continue to feed,
And I know He'll give the blessing you need.

God will supply all your needs every day.
God will lead you in peace as you travel His way.
God will help you, in love, to keep Satan at bay.
Our God will supply all your needs.

Whenever you're tempted to quit or give up,
He'll come along side you and fill up your cup.
Whatever you're needing at that moment in time
Will be yours when you call on Christ's name divine.

God will supply all your needs every day.
God will lead you in peace as you travel His way.
God will help you, in love, to keep Satan at bay.
Our God will supply all your needs.

So never should you ever doubt, worry, fear
For our God is faithful and is always right near.
His power's availed when on Christ's name we call
For He has resources that outrank earth's all.

HEAVEN'S WISDOM

"But the wisdom that comes from heaven is first of all
pure; then peace-loving, considerate, submissive, full of
mercy and good fruit, impartial and sincere. Peacemakers
who sow in peace raise a harvest of righteousness."

James 3:17-18 NIV

The wisdom that comes from heaven
Is pure and seeks out peace-
Consideration for fellow man
With a love that should not cease.

The wisdom that comes from heaven
Submits for the common good.
It dies to self and lives for Christ.
It shows mercy, as it should.

The wisdom that comes from heaven
Good fruit is its renown.
This wisdom never chooses sides-
Impartiality's always shown.

The wisdom that comes from heaven
Does not wear a façade.
It is sincere and all can see
That this wisdom comes from God.

The wisdom that comes from heaven
Will be shown when peacemakers bless.
They will sow in peace and always raise
A harvest of righteousness.

HIERARCHY OF THE CALLED

A hierarchy does not exist
In those whom God has called.
No matter what you do for Christ,
There's no hierarchy at all.

A preacher who expounds the truth
To those lost on this earth
Holds the same rank as a laborer.
God's grace gives them same worth.

An evangelist who saves lost souls
And a doctor who saves lives -
If both perform their deeds for God,
No hierarchy divides.

All those who've called on Jesus' name
And received his love and grace
Will never have a brother raised
To a higher, more worthy place.

For all who know Christ as their Lord,
Their Redeemer, Savior, King
Are deemed the same in Jesus' eyes.
This truth in Scripture rings.

So do your deeds for Christ alone
As Scripture tells you to
And never think your deeds are less
Than those that others do.

HOSPITALITY

H is for the hands of Christ that we must use to serve.

O for opportunities if we will just observe.

S is sharing of our time and what else God provides.

P for protecting knowledge when someone in us confides.

I is the investment of resources and our time.

T for the treasures we'll discover most of times.

A for an attitude of serving, patterned after Christ.

L for love that is based on Christ, when He in us abides.

I is for the interest we take in others' lives.

T is trusting God to show you what you are to give.

Y by now, you've guessed stands for YOU, and only YOU

For only you can do the things that God wants you to do.

HOW COULD A KING?

Please tell me how the King of Kings
Could look on me with love.
How could He long for me to come
And show my love to prove

That He alone and no one else
Possessed my heart fore'er?
How could I tell Him that I long
My life, with Him, to share?

I run to Him with open arms
He holds His arms wide and says **"Come,
My love, my dearly loved one.
For now you have come home."**

I AM YOUR HANDIWORK

*"For you created my inmost being; you knit
me together in my mother's womb. I praise you
because I am fearfully and wonderfully made; your
works are wonderful, I know that full well."*

Psalm 139:13-14 NIV

I am your handiwork, designed by your hands
As a creation unique for all time.
There is no one just like me upon this earth.
That is so by your master design.
You knit me together in my mother's womb
And created my being within.
I praise you for I am wonderfully made
By my Redeemer, my Savior, my King.
Your works are wonderful; I know that full well.
I will tell all I meet what you've done.
You have not only given me physical birth
But second birth, through Christ Jesus, your son,
When His death brought me life and He bore all my sin
As He hung on the cross 'til He died.
But new life was only attained when He rose
And at your right hand now sits glorified.
So, I know that my physical birth was all planned
Long before this earth ever took shape,
And I pray that, in heaven, I will hear you say,
"I am pleased with the life that I made."

I CAN DO ALL THINGS

"I can do everything through him who gives me strength."

Philippians 4:13 NIV

I can walk on water, and ask mountains to move.
If I stay in the will of our King.
I can help feed the hungry in God's love and show
That in His power, I can do all things.

I can help the blind see the great love of God.
And I'll help the lame walk His way.
There's nothing I can do in my own strength;
So in God's strength, I know I must stay.

I can help all the blind who will not see the truth
I'll tell them what God's done for me.
That His love has given me grace, peace and joy
And over Satan, great victory.

I can plant the seeds of the truth of God's word,
And maybe I'll see the seeds sprout.
And God, in his great grace, may allow me to reap
A harvest for Him, Kingdom-bound.

Knowing His faithfulness, and what His word says,
I anticipate what life may bring.
Because I'm sustained and held secure in his care,
I know I can do anything.

I KNOW HE LIVES

*I know that my redeemer lives, and that in
the end he will stand on the earth.*

Job 19.25 NIV

I know that my Redeemer lives
And, on this earth, He'll stand.
The day that He comes back again
Will be glorious and grand.
He will not come in flesh and blood
As when He walked this earth;
He won't come helpless as a babe
As on the morning of His birth.
He'll come in power and majesty,
In control of all He sees.
Where'er He looks, the people there
Will be falling on their knees.
Their voices will proclaim Him Lord,
Against their will or not,
And all believers will rejoice
For their souls, with blood, He bought.

I KNOW YOU'RE NEAR

When the world stirs around me
And tries to make me fall,
No harm will happen to me
When on your name I call.
I know you'll never leave me;
Your word told me that truth.
No crown or principality
Can overpower you.
I know you're ever mindful
And watch my every step,
And in your loving kindness
My life is daily kept.
You'll guide my waking moments;
You'll guard me as I sleep.
I'll rest in quiet assurance
That your promises you'll keep.
And when life's tempo spins too fast,
And I cannot stand the pace,
It's then I know I will be safe,
For I'll rest within your grace.
Your power is availed to me
In daytime or in night;
I have but to call out your name
To experience your might.
What man can stand against you
In his human feeble strength?
I'll draw just what I need from you
When my human strength is spent.
So, Lord, as we walk hand in hand
Along life's path each day,
I thank you for your love and grace
As I walk your narrow way.

I LOVE YOU; YOU HAVE WORTH

One day I had a vision. The dream it was so real.
My Father spoke from heaven. His loving I could feel.
"My child, I love you dearly. To me you have great worth.
My love will e'er be with you, no matter where on earth
Your life's road takes you. With you, I'll walk beside
Until I call you home, Child, and you with me reside.
We'll walk and talk together – no pain, no trials, no tears –
I'll hear you sing my praises throughout the endless years.
For now, you must remain there – on Earth – to do my task.
I know that you'll obey me, no matter what I ask.
You'll show to all the people you meet from day to day
The saving love I offer – I am the Light, the Way.
You'll share in all their gladness and share in all their tears.
They'll see my love shine through you, for all your numbered years.
And when I call you home, Child, to leave your time on earth,
You'll always hear me saying, "I love you; you have worth."

I REST SECURE

For I am convinced that neither death nor life, neither angels nor demons, neither the present nor the future, nor any powers, neither height nor depth, nor anything else in all creation, will be able to separate us from the love of God that is in Christ Jesus our Lord.

Romans 8:38-39

My heart is now convicted
That there's nothing on this earth
That will ever separate me
From the God who gives me worth.

No angel has the power,
No demon has the might
To ever separate me
For I rest within God's sight.

The present cannot do it;
The future time as well
Can't cleave the close communion
Since God saved my soul from hell.

No distance separates us;
No depths can ever cleave
For I know that Christ has saved me
And that He will never leave.

On this earth, there is not one thing
That can lure me from His hand
For God's love is all-sufficient.
This great truth I understand.

And I rest beside quiet waters
With the knowledge that's so great
That there's nothing in existence
That me, from God, can separate.

I STAND AMAZED

The mountains shout your majesty.
The wind whispers your praise.
The mighty trees, in praise to you,
Their lofty branches raise.
The squirrel in her cozy nest
Knows her Creator King,
And knows that He, in love for her,
Will provide everything.
The babbling brook whispers your name
As it gently flows along,
And different birds, in different lands,
All praise you with their song.
The lightning flashes 'You are King'
Across the darkened sky.
The thunder rolls at your command,
And clouds float up on high.

I stand in awe each time I see
Creation you have made.
Each thing a part of something else.
I watch and am amazed.
From simple flowers standing tall
In meadows lush and green
To mountain peaks that rise above
And worlds man has not seen.
The universe is so immense
Man has not seen the half
And yet he thinks he's done it all.
To hear that is to laugh.
I bow in adoration for
The great God that you are –
Sustainer of all you have made
In all lands, near and far.

I WAS THE ONE

I was the one who betrayed you;
I kissed you there on the cheek.
I was the one who hewed out the cross
That caused you to fall to your knees.

I was the one who hammered the nails.
I pierced your hands, feet and side.
If I was the one who did all these things,
Then why was it you, Christ, that died?

I WILL PRAISE YOU, O LORD

I will praise you, O LORD, with all my heart; I will tell of all your wonders. I will be glad and rejoice in you; I will sing praise to your name, O Most High.

Psalm 9:1-2 NIV

I will praise you, O LORD, with all of my heart.
I will speak of the wonders you've done.
I'll rejoice and be glad in you, O my Lord,
For you're the Father's own precious Son.
I'll sing praise to your name till eternity's past
For the love that you've given to me.
All my enemies stumble and perish, O LORD,
When your power and might they can see.
You've upheld my cause and you've upheld my right –
Righteous judgment comes from your throne.
You've rebuked the nations and the wicked destroyed,
And their names now in history aren't known.
The Lord reigns forever; He's established his throne
And in righteousness He forever will reign
With justice, He will govern the lands of the earth,
And in love, He'll remove sin's dark stain.
The LORD is the refuge for all the oppressed.
A refuge in times of great strife.
Those who call on your name will trust you, O LORD,
For you're the one that can sustain all life.
You have never forsaken, as it says in your Word.
On this promise I know I can stand.
For no matter the time or my life's circumstance,
I believe that I'm held in your hand.
I will praise you, O LORD, with all of my heart.
I will speak of the wonders you've done.
I'll rejoice and be glad in you, O my Lord,
For you're the Father's own precious Son.

I WILL SING TO THE LORD

I will sing to the LORD, for he has been good to me.

Psalm 13:6 NIV

I will sing to the Lord because he's been so good to me,
Gave me love, peace and joy and a hope for eternity.
His praises I'll sing 'til my body can't draw a breath,
All glory and honour until my eyes are closed in death.

I will sing to the Lord because he's been so good to me,
Took the scales off my eyes so that I now can clearly see.
I'll sing of the grace that was to me so freely given,
And continue that song when my soul wings its way to heaven.

I will sing to the Lord because he's been so good to me.
He loved me enough that he died there on Calvary.
The crown made of thorns that was meant for my mortal head,
Jesus wore out of love that was proved by each drop he bled.

I will sing to the Lord because he's been so good to me,
Cleansed my soul, gave new life and The Lord set my spirit free.
No longer in bondage, I know that I'm not alone
For the Lord is beside me, no matter where I may roam.

IN THE SHADOW OF CALVARY'S CROSS

When I stand in the shadow of Calvary's cross
I know that my sins are no more
For the blood that was shed has ensured I am saved
And my kinship with Christ is restored.

And I'll sing alleluias to Jesus, my King,
Who willingly went to the cross
So that sinners like me who were condemned to die
Would no longer be damned and be lost.

And I'll tell of Christ's great love for all of mankind
And I'll tell of God's divine plan
To deliver to earth in the form of a child
The bridge between heaven and man.

A child who would grow and begin God's great work
To cleanse and to sanctify all
Who would admit they were sinners and truly repent
And on God's holy name they would call.

So I'll stay in the shadow of Calvary's cross
And my thanks to the Lord I will raise
For the love that he showed when he suffered and died.
God and Christ are owed all my praise!

JOURNEY TO SALVATION

I walked up to God's mercy seat
And repented of my sin.
The Lord looked down and took my hand
And cleansed my heart within.

I did not think me worthy
Of such a gift of grace,
But God, in his great mercy,
Gave me a royal place.

Tho' folks who look upon me
The change can never see,
I know that Christ, my savior,
Forgave and renewed me.

My heart is his abode now.
I know he'll never leave.
And through my lifetime on this earth
Forever, I'll believe.

LET ME HEAR YOUR VOICE, LORD

If, at any given moment,
I will have to make a choice
To walk your way or not, Lord,
Please let me hear your voice.

The world will try to tempt me
With abundant wealth and fame.
But they will not prevail, Lord,
If I call upon your name.

Men will say it does not matter
If I follow you or not.
But I know the truth, dear Jesus,
And won't give their words a thought.

I'll tell them of the sacrifice
As you hung there in my place,
That Calvary was the setting
For God's great amazing grace.

That a sinner was reborn there
And a life was made brand new
When I came with my repentant heart
And surrendered all to you.

So, Jesus, let me heed your voice;
Let me never turn away.
From the narrow path to glory's gate
May my footsteps never stray.

LETTER TO A MOTHER

When my Savior lived at your house,
Did he jump and run and play?
Did He ask a zillion questions?
Did you know just what to say?

Did He ask why clouds are fluffy?
Why the birds know what to sing?
Did He ask where babies come from?
Just what did you tell my King?

Did my Lord come running to you
When he fell and skinned his knee?
Did you cleanse and make it better,
Like He cleansed my soul for me?

At the end of the day, Mary,
As He lay against your breast,
Did He throw His arms around you
And say "Mommy, I love you best."?

Did you watch Him grow to manhood
While He did His Father's will?
Did you store those childhood memories
And wish that time would just stand still,

For you knew you'd see Him hanging,
On Golgotha, on the cross?
Did your comfort lied in knowing
That the world gained by your loss?

For He bore the sins of millions
When He died on Calvary's tree,
And you stood and watched Him suffer
To ensure new life for me.

So I'd like to thank you, Mary,
For your part in my Christ's life.
I will try to be more like you
As a mother and a wife.

I will use your love and patience
As examples of the best,
And we'll sit and talk together
When I go Home to rest.

LIVING WATER

Jesus answered, "Everyone who drinks this water will be thirsty again, but whoever drinks the water I give him will never thirst. Indeed, the water I give him will become in him a spring of water welling up to eternal life."

John 4:13-14 NIV

If you have the living water,
Then you'll never thirst again.
If you'll drink the living water
You'll be cleansed of all your sin.

When you drink the living water,
(On this fact you can depend)
It will become a spring of water
That will never find an end.

And the spring that wells within you
Eternal life, to you, will give
And you'll praise God as through each day
The Father's narrow way you live.

Living water's what I long for!
Living water's what I need!
Let this water flow right through me
So that all the world will see.

MUSTARD SEED FAITH

Sometimes the world can be so rough,
But I know I'll make it through
For, if I rest within your will,
There's nothing I can't do.
The mountain <u>will</u> walk to the sea;
Your word tells me that truth
If I but have that mustard seed
Of faith because of you.
The giant <u>will</u> fall at my feet,
Like David did of old.
The lion's mouth will be shut tight;
I'll stand up firm and bold.
And when my oil jar runs dry,
My light will still shine clear
For you'll provide all that I need.
I'll rest in peace, not fear.
For when you're near, all that is small
And seen of no import
Becomes a thing that you can use
And claim forevermore.
When on my own, I can do naught.
But when you're by my side,
I can be used by you, dear Lord,
If I, in you, abide.
So, Lord, take all I am and have
And use me as you would.
I'll follow where you lead, my Lord,
Your word has said I should.

MY HOPE IS IN THE LORD

In whom do I hope? I hope in the Lord,
For I love his promise written down in his Word.
A life of abundance, a life filled with peace,
A life filled with love that I know will not cease.
He will never leave me; he'll never forsake.
My God has the power and might it will take
To calm all the storms of life that appear
The reason I hope on God is quite clear.

And why do I hope? Well, I know in the past
His faithfulness proves that his promise will last
Throughout stormy weather and days full of sun.
He'll walk right beside me 'til my days are done.
No matter what circumstance comes into my life,
No matter the troubles, no matter the strife,
My God will prove faithful throughout all my days,
And for this great faithful God, I've nothing but praise.

NAME ABOVE ALL NAMES

"Therefore God exalted him to the highest place and gave him the name that is above every name, that at the name of Jesus every knee should bow, in heaven and on earth and under the earth, and every tongue confess that Jesus Christ is Lord, to the glory of God the Father."

Philippians 2:9-11

To the highest place Christ was exalted
And God gave him the name.
The name that's above all other names
For no other's quite the same.

At Jesus's name, every knee should bow
In heaven, on earth too.
Under the earth and in every place,
Christ will get his due.

Every tongue will confess that Jesus is Lord,
They will not have a choice.
The weak and the mighty, the rich and the poor
Will acclaim Christ with one voice.

And all will be done to the glory of God,
Our Father who sits on high.
When the earth acknowledges Christ as Lord,
All will see His power and might.

OUT OF THE DARKNESS

"But you are not like that, for you are a chosen people. You are royal priests, a holy nation, God's very own possession. As a result, you can show others the goodness of God, for he called you out of darkness into his wonderful light.

1 Peter 2:9 NIV

I stepped out of the darkness and into the light.
I walked into the day and out of the night.
Called by our Savior as holy and pure.
God's own possession, we are assured.
Because of His favor, God's goodness we'll show
So that all the world's lost will witness and know
That each one is loved by our Father on high.
Christ's death on Calvary, their freedom did buy.
No more will they ever be enslaved by sin,
If they will but let God, our Father, within.
And fear will be replaced with joy and with peace,
And God's love and mercy that will never cease.
Into each of their lives, He will impart His grace,
And the Son-shine will cause all the darkness to fade.

PROMISES MADE, PROMISES KEPT

*"I am with you and will watch over you wherever you go,
and I will bring you back to this land. I will not leave
you until I have done what I have promised you."*

Genesis 28:15 NIV

When man makes a promise, there's always a chance
That it won't be completed, or not come to pass.
But you, Lord, have always been faithful and true.
Whatever you say, Lord, then that's what you do.
You said that you'll never forsake me or leave;
I know in my heart I can firmly believe.
I'll walk through this world with assurance held strong
That, no matter the trial, you'll walk right along.
You said that I'll never be snatched from your grasp;
I rest in that fact, Lord. What more can I ask?
You said when I yield up my repentant heart
A life of abundance, in you, I will start.
Abundance not known by the world in its time
But abundance of grace, love and mercy is mine.
Grace that will pardon, and mercy unearned,
Love without boundaries. This fact I have learned.
You said that when time comes that death shuts my eyes,
My soul will soar heav'nward, above the blue skies
And I'll join all the angels in chorus of praise
For the promises kept and the promises made.

RIGHTEOUS, FAITHFUL, LOVING AND JUST

"For the word of the LORD is right and true; he is faithful in all he does. The LORD loves righteousness and justice; the earth is full of his unfailing love."

Psalm 33:4-5 NIV

For the word of the LORD is truthful and right;
He is faithful in all that He does.
Justice and righteousness are loved by the LORD;
The world's full of His unfailing love.

He's righteous and holy, and faithful as well
As we read in His holy word.
All knowing, all present, and all powerful, too,
Are attributes of this great LORD.

His love has no measure; his power has no end.
These things will be forever true.
God's plan of salvation involved death on the cross,
But Christ did it for me and for you.

There's no past or present, no thought, word or deed
No act that, in sin, you have done
Will stop God from loving you from the moment you yield
Your repentant heart to His son.

And your heart will be filled with His great peace,
And your life will be filled with His grace.
His mercy and love will surround you
Until you meet Him in heaven, face to face.

SAVED FROM SATAN, SANCTIFIED BY A SAVIOR

Satan had me bound in chains
Of doubt and deep despair.
He told me that I walked alone
Without a hope or prayer.
I listened to the temptor's lies;
My life was filled with dross.
But then a friend spoke of a King
Who died on Calvary's cross.
A King who treasured me so much
That He walked to death that day.
A Savior, who is Jesus Christ –
The Life, the Truth, the Way.
And all I need do to receive
The blessings He affords
Is call on His name and proclaim
Him as my King and Lord.
What joy replaced the doubt and fear!
What peace my heart now knew!
The love of Christ will never leave
And will be ever true.
Each day He gives me what I need;
I rest within His care.
We have communion through His word
And in my hour of prayer.
And with the knowledge of God's love
No power does Satan hold,
For I know now, through God's own words,
Satan's fate has been foretold.
And no man or throne or kingdom
Can pluck me from God's hand.
I rest secure from any threat
When I live within His plan.

SLAVE TO MY SAVIOUR

I'm a slave for my Saviour.
I am free but bound close.
His death gave me new life
This redeemed sinner knows.

My chains aren't of iron,
But pure links of grace,
Bestowed by my Saviour
When He died in my place.

Those shackles constrain me
To walk in His way,
In each waking moment
And throughout every day.

Most slaves dream of freedom
But I'm free in my chains.
I choose now to wear them;
My choice is quite plain.

The chain length grows daily
As I see every day
God's great love and mercy
That to me is displayed.

His faithfulness forges
A new link or two;
With each faithful moment
His great love He proves.

I'm a slave to my Saviour
I wear his chains with pride
For I know it was for me
That on Calv'ry He died.

THE HEAVENS DECLARE GOD'S GLORY

Psalm 19

The heavens declare God's glory.
The skies proclaim his acts.
Day after day, they pour forth speech.
Nightly, they display his facts.
There is no speech or no language
Where their voice cannot be heard.
Their voice goes out into the earth.
Their words to the end of the world.
He has pitched a tent in the heavens
For the sun, and what is more,
Is it's like a bridegroom coming
Or a champion running a course.
From the eastern end of the heavens
It journeys and sets in the west.
Nothing escapes from its great heat;
To try would make one hard pressed.
The law of the LORD is perfect,
And a soul will be revived.
His laws are ever trustworthy
And the simple are made wise.
Right are all of his precepts;
They give joy unto the heart.
Radiant are his laws and commands
And the eyes contain a spark.
So, pure is the fear of the LORD and
Forever it will endure.
He is altogether righteous
And his ordinances are sure.
His laws are more precious than pure gold
And honeycomb's never as sweet.
By them one's given a warning,
And a reward that just can't be beat.

61

Who can discern the LORD's errors?
Forgive my hidden faults.
Keep me away from willful sins
So my loyalty cannot be bought.
Then will I become blameless,
Innocent of any great sin.
So throughout my earthly life, LORD,
In communion we'll enter in.
May all the thoughts of my heart, LORD,
And all of the words that I speak
Be pleasing in your holy sight, LORD,
The Rock and Redeemer I seek.

THE LORD'S NAME IS A TOWER

The name of the LORD is a strong tower;
the righteous run to it and are safe.

Proverbs 18:9-11 NIV

The Lord's name is a tower;
The righteous know its power
And run to it in times of strife.
Its strength cannot be matched;
The righteous know this fact.
That information saves their life.

All enemies defeated,
All evil force retreated,
We praise our God for what He's done.
We stand upon the tower,
In triumph and God's power
Exalting God and Christ, his Son.

No might or circumstance
Can wrest us from God's hands.
We abide in Him and rest secure.
If we stay in the tower,
Every minute of each hour,
Each trial we will surely endure.

THE MARRIAGE CORD

A cord of three strands cannot easily be broken;
Its strength is derived in the fact that there's three.
The first two cords are the wife and her husband,
And Jesus, the Savior, is the third cord, you see.

Each strand is important so the marriage is successful.
Each one is unique in the qualities it brings.
The husband and wife bring their love for each other,
And the blessing's bestowed by Jesus, the King.

When the troubles of life cause one strand to unravel,
There's always two others to heal and restore.
The troubles are shared and the victories increased
When the husband and wife both know Jesus as Lord.

When the husband and wife share a love of the Savior,
When the reading of Scripture in their home is heard,
Then the richest of blessings will be heaped upon them,
As they live, every moment, in God's glorious Word.

As we've seen in these moments of vows and exchanged rings,
The bride and her bridegroom have a new marriage cord;
To sustain it, both spouses have to love one another
And continue to love, trust and obey the Lord.

It's only then they'll see God's truest blessings upon them;
It's only then that they both will continue to see
God's grace and His mercy and love everlasting
As they live and they love in a cord made of three.

THE PERFECT GIFT

I walked along the darkened streets;
The stores were locked up tight.
My search for that elusive gift
Had taken half the night,
And yet I had not found the gift
My heart was searching for.
I felt that gift would not be mine
For I had searched each store.

But then I gazed up at the sky
And saw the twinkling star.
My mind recalled that Bible tale
Of wise men from afar
That followed such a star until
It settled o'er the place
Where Jesus lay on manger bed
And shepherds bowed their face.

That Bible tale had told of Christ
Who'd die upon the cross
To fulfill God's salvation plan
And save mankind, all lost.
'Twas then I knew what needed done
To find that gift so rare.
I only had to yield my heart
Into the Savior's care.

I knew that He would never leave;
I'd never be alone.
I knew His love would drive out fear
And His blood for sin atone.
The gift I got that darkened night
Will never fade away.
I have the love of Jesus Christ,
The Truth, the Life, the Way.

THE SEED AND THE SOILS

While a large crowd was gathering and people were coming to Jesus from town after town, he told this parable: "A farmer went out to sow his seed. As he was scattering the seed, some fell along the path; it was trampled on, and the birds ate it up. Some fell on rocky ground, and when it came up, the plants withered because they had no moisture. Other seed fell among thorns, which grew up with it and choked the plants. Still other seed fell on good soil. It came up and yielded a crop, a hundred times more than was sown."

Luke 8:4-8 NIV

A farmer went out to sow his seed.
And it fell on different ground.
And though the seed was all the same
Different results there were found.

Some fell along the path and then
Were trampled under foot.
The birds then feasted on the seed,
And it could do no good.

Some fell on very rocky ground,
And when the plants grew high,
Without a source of moisture there,
They withered and they died.

And other seed fell among thorns,
That grew up with the seed.
The thorns grew strong and choked the plants
And the plants succumbed to the weeds.

Still other seed fell on fertile ground,
The advantage clearly shown.
From each seed came a hundredfold,
A lot more than was sown.

The disciples asked, "Lord, what's it mean?
We cannot understand."
The Lord said, "What it clearly shows
Is the Word and the way of man.

The seed is an image of God's Word,
And the ground is how it grows.
The different ground makes the difference for
The seed is the same, you know.

The first seed fell along the path;
The word in a person's heart.
But the devil came and stole the seed
And the plant's growth could not start.

The second seed fell on rocky ground;
The seed was received with joy.
But it didn't grow roots that reached far down,
And, in times of trials, was destroyed.

The third seed fell among the thorns;
The thorns are life's worry and cares.
When the seeds grew together, the thorns prevailed
And the seed could not flourish there.

The last seed fell on fertile ground;
It persevered and grew strong and well -
From one little seed, a hundred or more.
Do you understand now what I tell?"

Oh, Lord, now that your Word's in my heart,
Please ensure that I'm grounded in you.
Don't let all of life's worries steal what I have.
Help my faith to grow deep and stay true.

THE SWINGING DOOR

Death's door swings into heaven,
A glorious land unknown
Where praise and laud and honour
Are to Christ Jesus shown -
A land where paths are golden
And sorrows don't exist.
Where tears are wiped away in love
And doubt and fear desist.
What joy will we experience
As we journey from life's shore!
What peace to know at all times
That we'll depart no more
From the precious love of Jesus
As we're held in His embrace!
What ecstasy when finally
We see Christ face-to-face!
Eternity will find us
In that joyful praising throng
Of all the saints who've gone before.
We'll join their grateful song.

Death's door swings into Hades
A land of pain and grief
Where wailing sounds surround one.
Our minds cannot conceive!
The darkness will encompass
Each soul that has been lost,
For each soul that resides there
Will pay the awful cost
Of earthly lives lived just for self
Without a thought for God,
Of lives consumed with earthly gain
Who never offered laud

To God and His son, Jesus
Their creator and earth's King.
To stop their tortured daily lives
They cannot do a thing.
The fire, ever hungry,
Will burn but not consume.
A earthly life lived without God
Will seal those poor souls' doom.

So choose today the life you lead.
Be conscious of one thing:
The life you live while here on earth
Will chart where death's door swings.

THE WORLD OR THE WORD

"Sitting down, Jesus called the Twelve and said, "If anyone wants to be first, he must be the very last, and the servant of all."

Mark 9:35 NIV

The world says that you are your own inner god.
Don't care for the person on whose back you trod.
Don't care for the others that fall 'neath your quest.
Don't see them as people, just believe you are best.
It says you're entitled to have all you can
Without ever thinking of your fellow man.

The Word says that you have a great inner God.
You must care for each person wherever you trod.
And care for the others that you find in your quest
To see them as people and show them God's best.
You are no more entitled than your fellow man.
You must bring them the light of God's salvation plan.

So choose now your master, the world or the Word.
Your place on the world's stage, or days with the Lord.
For if the world is your choice, then Friend please understand
On earth all your rewards will be given by man.
But if the Word is your choice, then your just reward
Will be eternity spent praising the Lamb, Christ the Lord.

THERE IS NO GOD LIKE YOU

No creation, no throne or no kingdom
Can give love that's so precious and true.
I know that a created god-thing
Can never compare, Lord, to you.
For the eyes of the idol looks forward
And its ears cannot hear any prayer.
Tell me, how can I wooden creation
Protect people who are left in its care?
But you, Lord, look over earth's framework,
You made it before time began.
You created the beasts, plants and birds, Lord,
And from dust, in your image, made man.
When man makes a choice to reject you
How it must make your heart almost break!
For the temporal things of the world, Lord,
The eternal and you they forsake.
But when repentant hearts call on you, Lord,
And confess all their sins in your name,
Then the peace, joy and love that you offer
And eternity's promise they'll claim.

THRONE OF GLORY, THRONE OF GRACE

When my old ship was sinking fast
I knew my vessel could not last
Against the waves that o'er me crashed
But God reached down his hand.

And when the Savior took my hand
I then began to understand
That the throne of glory became my throne of grace.

He pulled me from the heaving waves
I know that Christ's the one that saves
To heaven's door the way He paved
For God reached down his hand.

And when the Savior took my hand
I then began to understand
That the throne of glory became my throne of grace.

I'll sail my ship with his commands
On his great words I'll ever stand
For all my life the Savior planned
When God reached down his hand.

And when the Savior took my hand
I then began to understand
That the throne of glory became my throne of grace.

UNDER NEW MANAGEMENT

Unless the Lord builds the house, its builders labor in vain.

Psalm 127:1 NIV

Oh, Father, take this house of mine.
You've bought it and it's wholly thine.
The bill of sale was signed in red
With blood that flowed from Jesus' head,
With blood that flowed from hands and feet
That made salvation's plan complete.
And if you think it need be, Lord,
Demolish, Father, board by board.
And though I may not understand
I know it is your master plan.
With brooms of truth, sweep out the dirt
Each painful moment, every hurt,
So, in the end, the world will see
Your handiwork displayed in me.
Shine up the windows of my heart
So that the world will see the start
Of something special, something new –
Each room designed in love by you.
And though my plan was not as grand,
I revel in your master plan.
A house in disrepair and grime
Became a palace for all time.

WHAT IS THE COLOUR OF LOVE?

Red is the colour of love, you see.
Christ really proved his great love for me
When his blood flowed down from the old rugged tree.
Red is the colour of love, you see.

Black is the colour of love, I know.
Christ on the cross his great love did show
When he cleansed my sin-darkened soul white as snow.
Black is the colour of love, I know.

White is the colour of love, it's plain
My life will never be the same again
Because my Lord turned to white my ebony stain.
White is the colour of love, it's plain

On Calvary's hilltop, these colours met.
A day that the world should never forget.
Red blood made white all my sin, black as jet.
Christ is the colour of love, you bet.

WHEN I ASKED FOR FORGIVENESS

Forgive us our debts, as we have forgiven our debtors.

Matthew 6:12 NIV

You did not use the words of scorn
That all my sins were worth.
You merely took me in your arms
And gave me second birth.

You did not say "You foolish child!"
When I confessed my sin.
You never turned your face away
Or said, "Never again!!"

You never left me in my shame.
No derisive words were said.
Instead, a covenant was made
And signed in crimson red.

A covenant whose words I love
Whose truth I daily take.
And if I walk in love with you
You'll never leave me nor forsake.

So help me, Lord, to show your love
To forgive, and do the same
As what you did when I confessed
And called upon your name.

WHEN MY WORLD FALLS DOWN AROUND ME

When my world falls down around me
And lies in pieces I can't mend,
That's the time you lend your power.
On this fact I can depend.

And I know there's not an issue
You can't handle in your might,
But you wait until I call you
And that's when you make it right.

For you wait 'til I acknowledge
That without you, I am lost.
Then you pick up all the pieces
And make a masterpiece from dross.

For it's only then I realize
That without you in my life,
I would never have your comfort
As I suffered pain and strife.

And the grace you offer to me,
As a gift bestowed so free
Is the one thing I require
For my own soul's liberty.

So, Lord, always keep my focus
Fixed on you until my end,
And I thank you for the promise
That on you I can depend.

WHO CAN SEPARATE US FROM THE LOVE OF CHRIST?

"Who shall separate us from the love of Christ? Shall trouble or hardship or persecution or famine or nakedness or danger or sword? No, in all these things we are more than conquerors through him who loved us."

Romans 8:35,37 NIV

Who can separate us from the love of Christ?
The answer's in His word.
Not trouble or hardship, not famine or strife
Can cleave us from the Lord.
Nakedness or danger don't have the power
To take us from His hand.
For the power rests in the Savior's right hand
A truth we understand.
We will be the victors who wait on the Lord
No fear within our hearts.
With the knowledge of His compassionate love
Peace and joy His love imparts.
And through Christ 's blood shed on Calvary's cross
Our victory is great,
And from the love of our dear Lord, Jesus Christ,
Nothing can us separate.

WITH GOD AT MY SIDE

When I alone confront my foes,
I cannot hope to stand.
But with my God right at my side
I'm saved by his strong hand.

No king or principality
Prevails when God is near.
For with my God right at my side
I have no need to fear.

There is no time or circumstance
When he will not be there.
And with my God right at my side
I'm sheltered in his care.

What more could mortal man desire?
What peace his presence brings!
For with my God right at my side
I can do anything.